INSIDE MUM

To our daughters
Marguerite and Suzannah

INSIDE MUM

An illustrated account of conception,
pregnancy and childbirth

By Sylvia Caveney
Pictures by Simon Stern

SIDGWICK & JACKSON

First published in 1976 by Sidgwick and Jackson Limited
Copyright © 1976 by Sylvia Caveney and Simon Stern

Special thanks to Dr Tim Gordon and Mr P. J. Humphries

ISBN 0 283 98247 0

Printed in Great Britain by
A. Wheaton & Co., Exeter
for Sidgwick and Jackson Limited
1 Tavistock Chambers, Bloomsbury Way
London WC1A 2SG

Contents

Where did I come from?

Maybe you know the story of the boy who asked his mother,

"Where did I come from?"

"The Doctor brought you in his little black bag," she said.

"How about you and Dad?"

"The stork brought us."

"Well, what happened with Grannie and Grandpa then?"

"They were found under a gooseberry bush."

So the boy went back to school and wrote in his Biology Book,

"There has not been a normal birth in our family for three generations."

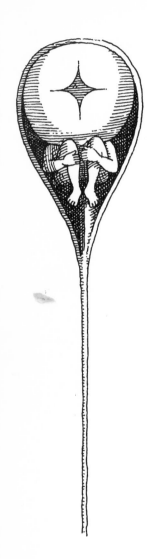

Homunculists thought each sperm held a tiny baby which grew to full size in the womb.

We have all heard this sort of story—maybe you know a better one. This one is funny because it's so true. In the past people made a mystery of child-bearing, perhaps because it is a mystery in the old sense of being a miracle, perhaps because having a child is an intensely private emotional experience and not something that's easy to talk about. There is, too, a tradition of giggles and embarrassment which it's hard to break through.

As well as being funny, the story shows how ideas change. The mother was fobbed off with stories and nonsense; her son learns the biological facts at school.

Twentieth-century childbirth isn't less miraculous, or less full of feeling. There's a more open view of childbirth as an ordinary event, quite reasonably when you consider every one of the world's population arrives more or less the same way.

One reason for this more open view is that twentieth-century scientists have found out what really goes on. Before that some very strange ideas were about. Until 1759 no one realized that a male cell joined a female cell to make a child. The Ovists thought a mother's ovary held a complete but very tiny baby which started growing when set off by the male sperm. The Homunculists said that sperm contained a miniature child, all curled up, which grew in the mother like a seed in a plant-pot.

Pythagoras got his theorems right, but his idea that vapour from the man's brain and nerves made an egg which he passed on to a woman was definitely wrong.

It's great fun to look at these old ideas, and to see that now, for the first time in history, we can give the right answer to the question we all ask, "Where do babies come from?"

Samoan children enjoy watching a birth. The village children rush to the hut where a new baby is arriving. In Bali, children think that the witches who wait to snatch the new born child might snatch them too, so they hide. Bornu girls can help the other women make the baby beautiful by stroking and pressing it with warmed hands, and in south west Nigeria any girl can be present at a birth so long as she is older than the mother. Some modern hospitals don't allow children to see their mother and the new baby in case of infection. Which set-up do you think you would prefer?

Conception: how you began

A child begins when a sperm reaches the living tissue inside an *egg cell* (the *ovum*).

Women carry the egg cells, about a quarter of a million of them, in their *ovaries* or "eggeries". Each month one egg ripens, and is sent out along the *fallopian tube*.

Men produce the sperm, 300 million or so at a time, in the round organs called the *testes*. The bag which holds them hangs outside the body, so the sperm are stored at a temperature slightly cooler than body temperature.

Sperm travel upwards, the ovum travels down. To make a new life they must meet in the right place—the fallopian tube—at the right time.

Earlier or later will not do.

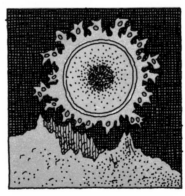

A ripe egg bursts out of the ovary at the start of its journey. If it is not fertilized it dies and melts away.

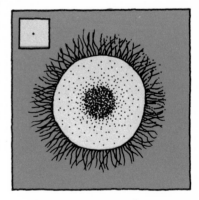

The egg is spun round by the thousands of sperm swarming round it, lashing their tails, and trying to penetrate it. Once the egg is fertilized, its surface seals over so no other sperm can enter.

Inset: The egg—actual size.

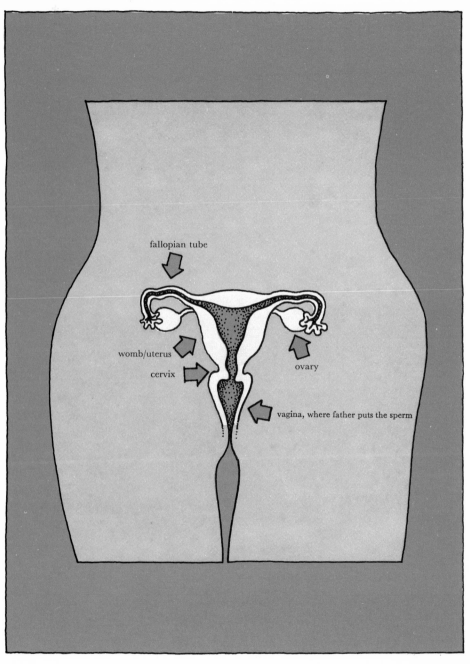

fallopian tube

womb/uterus

cervix

ovary

vagina, where father puts the sperm

This diagram shows the reproductory organs—those to do with producing babies—inside a woman.

12

Though lots of sperm are lost on the way, thousands reach the egg and try to penetrate it. Some get as far as the outer layers, but finally one gets through to the nucleus, then the two cells stop being a sperm and an egg, and become one single cell.

This is the moment of conception. In this fraction of a second is decided who this child will be, boy or girl, tall or short, dark or fair. Every physical feature is there, ready and waiting to grow.

The path of the ripe egg; it leaves the ovary, passes along the fallopian tube, is fertilized, and divides on the way to the womb where it implants itself.

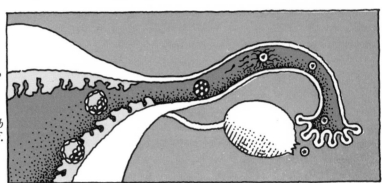

The egg is about half the size of a pinhead. Sperm are much smaller; you would need 2,500 to cover a pinhead. Their vital meeting happens in a tube as thick as a bristle from your hairbrush.

The egg is now fertile, it can produce life, and it starts growing straight away. Thirty hours later it has divided into two cells. These two divide into four, the four make eight, then sixteen, then thirty-two and so on.

All this time it goes on travelling down the fallopian tube toward the womb. After three days it has more than 100 cells. By the time it's a baby ready to be born it will have more than 200 billion.

After 30 hours the ovum has 2 cells. It goes on growing and dividing, and after 7 days the 150 cells separate into two groups: cells to form the child, and cells to form the placenta.

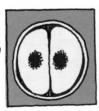   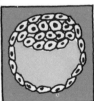

Fertility, the possibility of new life, is important in every part of nature. Without it there would be no new plants or animals or people. Many religions have gods or goddesses of fertility, and have festivals at springtime and harvest.

People want children for many reasons; in poorer countries, parents expect children to care for them in old age; in richer countries they hope children will carry on the family name, and with it, something of themselves into the future.

Sadly not everyone is fertile. About 10 per cent of couples can't produce children, though they may be helped by doctors and drugs.

Until the early twentieth century people expected to have lots of children though most of them died. This still happens in poor countries, but where good health care makes almost every child survive, people think it better to have only those children they really want and can look after. So as well as helping the childless, doctors are asked to help the fertile find ways of *contraception*—avoiding the conception of unwanted children.

The Greek God Dionysus holds an egg and a cockerel, symbols of fertility and rebirth. In the past, infertile wives tried magic as much or more than they tried medicine. Roman doctors in the second century hung wives upside down on a ladder for twenty-four hours, then gave them cold barley water. Elizabethans drank cat-mint tea or sage juice.

The foetus at 1 day and 28 days—actual size.
At 28 days it is 10,000 times bigger than the first
single cell. It has a head fold and a tail fold, arm
and leg buds, eyes and nose and the beginnings of a
brain, spinal cord and backbone—all in a blob of
jelly 1 cm long.

The first month of life

Every month the womb gets ready to receive a fertile egg, and makes a lining of rich blood cells. Most often the egg is not fertilized, so the lining is broken up and shed. This is the cycle known as *menstruation* or the monthly *period*, or even the *"curse"*, and it lasts four or five days.

So, when a fertile egg comes down the fallopian tube, the womb is ready for it.

By the time the egg reaches the womb it is 5 or 6 days old, and a round ball of about 150 cells. It separates into two layers. The outer layer buries itself in the womb lining where it will make the *placenta* and *umbilicus* to supply the growing baby with food and oxygen. The inner layer of larger cells will form the child's body.

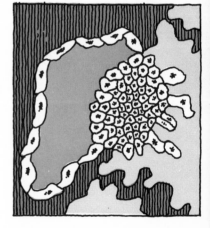

The egg implants itself in the womb lining around the seventh day.

15

We call the bundle of cells a *foetus* or *embryo*—the Latin and Greek words for developing child.

At two weeks old the foetus would fit easily on your little finger nail. By four weeks it has grown a head and a tail fold, and buds of arms and legs. Its brain is appearing, and its backbone and spinal cord. It has eyes and nose, and a tiny heart just starting to beat—all this in a blob of jelly, 1 cm long and so soft it's hardly there at all.

Twenty-eight days ago it was a single cell the size of half a pinhead. In four weeks it's grown 10,000 times bigger. It will never change more or grow more rapidly in the whole of its life.

If the foetus went on growing at its present rate, it would be bigger than the world on its birth day.
In fact, the newly born child is a mere 6 billion times larger than the fertilized egg

Umbilicus and placenta

Altogether the foetus spends 36 weeks in the *uterus* or womb. The system for supplying food and oxygen is built between the 4th and 17th week.

When the egg's outer cells implanted themselves in the womb, some started forming the placenta, a layer of extra-rich blood cells, and some started the umbilicus, the cord that joins foetus and placenta.

Blood travels through the cord at 4 miles per hour—about an average walking speed—and it takes about 30 seconds for the round trip: placenta through cord, round baby, through cord, back to placenta.

Although the mother's circulation meets the child's at the placenta, their blood is quite separate and never mixes. The mother's blood brings oxygen and food to the placenta, but baby's blood takes it away, leaving wastes behind for the mother's blood to get rid of—clearing up after the baby even before it's born.

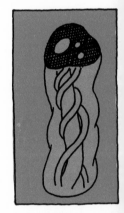

The umbilical cord has "in" and "out" veins for blood circulation.

Umbilicus and placenta start growing.

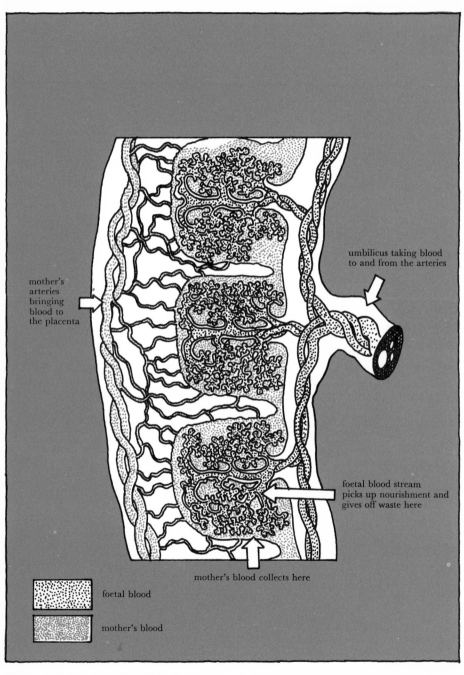

umbilicus taking blood
to and from the arteries

mother's
arteries
bringing
blood to
the placenta

foetal blood stream
picks up nourishment and
gives off waste here

mother's blood collects here

foetal blood

mother's blood

The mother's blood and foetal blood never mix.

Did you spot the gap in the system?

You read that in the first four weeks the foetus grew 10,000 times bigger, yet the placenta was working properly only around the 17th week.

What happened in between?

Well, the outermost layer of *morula* cells made a bag of permeable skin, that means skin which liquids can pass through, and food and oxygen filtered through it until the placenta and umbilicus took over.

When that happened, the skin, called *amnion*, started making a special liquid, and moved out to line the uterus, so that the foetus was inside a bag full of liquid.

Amnion is the Greek word for lamb, and is used to name this bag because lambs are usually born wrapped in theirs. The bag of amniotic fluid is a splendid protection for the baby. It keeps it warm and saves it from bangs and bumps. It's easy for the foetus to move about in, too. Just think how free and easy you feel when you're kicking about in the swimming pool.

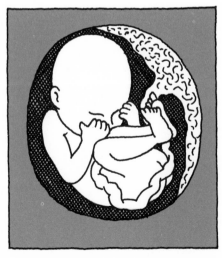

The fair-ground fish is saved from squashes and bumps by its bag of water, just as the foetus is cushioned by the amniotic fluid.

The six-week foetus—actual size.

6-10 weeks: arms and legs

Six weeks old and the foetus would fit comfortably into a walnut shell. It weighs rather less than a packet of book matches. Its heart, which started beating around the 25th day, keeps up a steady 65 beats a minute.

All the important organs are forming—those for dealing with food—stomach, liver and intestines; the lungs for breathing; the kidneys and bladder for getting rid of waste.

It's too early to see if this baby will be a boy or a girl, but the reproductive organs are growing; so, as early as this, the baby has the makings of its own children, the grandchildren of the mother it lies in.

The foetus is starting to look less like a tadpole and more like a baby, with a very broad face, wide-apart eyes, and a flat nose. Hearing and sight are growing in ears and eyes.

Its arms and legs grow amazingly fast. On the 24th day of life they are not there, two days later there are arm buds, and two days later leg buds. After another four days the buds have become arms and legs with the beginnings of toes and fingers.

21

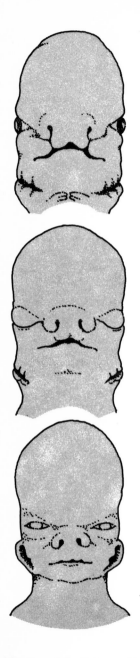

The face of the foetus—odd-looking little fellow, but recognizably human.

At eight weeks, the arms are the size of exclamation marks (!!) and have hands complete with fingers and thumbs. The legs have knees and ankles, and the feet have all their toes.

On palms and soles, the skin has already the distinctive patterns which don't change and are as unique as fingerprints. The muscles start to grow now, so the foetus can begin to move, but it's such a faint flickering the mother won't feel it.

So far the skeleton has been forming in soft gristle. During the 9th and 10th weeks the gristle starts to ossify, that is to change into bone. As the backbone ossifies, the foetus starts straightening its back.

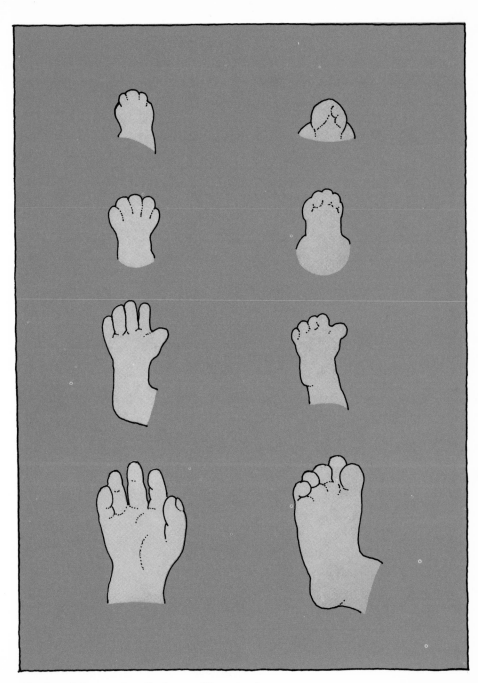

Hands and feet growing. See how at 7½ weeks the big toe sticks out as it does on an ape's foot—reminding us how our ape ancestors used their feet like hands.

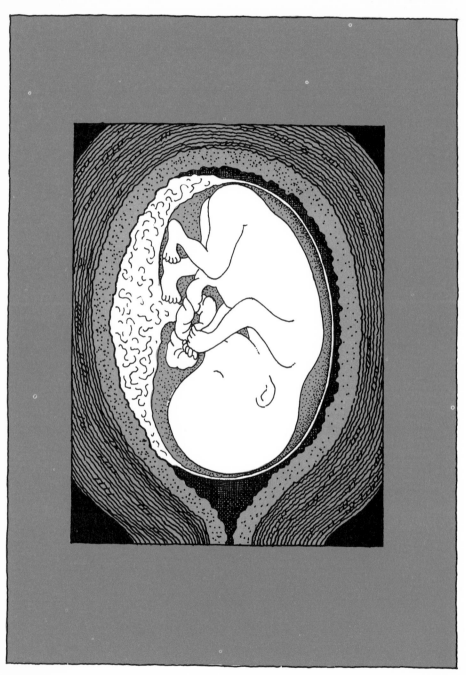

Twelve-week foetus—actual size

10-12 weeks: basic structure

When the foetus is ten weeks old the nervous system starts putting together a network that will link all parts of the body to the brain. The first links are formed at ten weeks, and if you could stroke this foetus with a feather you would find it ticklish everywhere except at the back of the head. This spot stays non-feeling until after birth.

The foetus uses its arms really well now, sweeping them round, and bending its elbows and wrists. At the end of each finger a nail is forming.

By the time the foetus is twelve weeks old its basic structure is finished. Although it weighs only an ounce/28 g, it has all the important organs, and from now on the changes are comparatively small ones. For example, in the next few weeks its head will straighten up and its brain work more strongly, and its vocal cords will soon be ready for talking and singing.

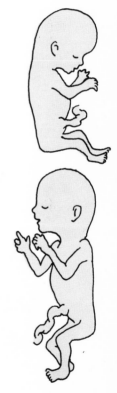

(*Above*) *The ten-week foetus moves its arms easily in the amniotic fluid. Its back is still curved.*
(*Below*) *The twelve-week foetus holds its head straighter, and can move fingers and thumbs as well as arms.*

At this stage its eyes will be sealed by eyelids. Many animals are born with eyes still sealed, kittens for instance, but the baby's eyes will open before birth. In the bones of its jaw 20 first-tooth buds appear.

It is getting better at moving now, and really quite graceful in the womb. The new muscles let it make small precise movements with fingers and thumbs.

At twelve weeks the baby's sex is distinguishable for the first time, and if you could see inside you would know if it was a boy or a girl. So, from now on we can stop calling the foetus "it" and say "him or her"—or, as that's rather long, we'll say "him" for short.

Pliny said, "Nature creates monsters to astonish us and amuse herself." Ambroise Paré, a famous 16th-century surgeon thought monsters were God's punishment, or were due to the Devil's interference. The picture of a bird-boy comes from his book—and his imagination.

Some old wives' tales have a grain of truth in them, but a once popular idea that women could give birth to animals or monsters was completely wrong.
In the 16th century Maria Tofts "gave birth" to several rabbits—once a week, in front of paying audiences. Business was good until the constable stepped in.
The embryo child can't be affected by what a mother sees, so there is no point in her dodging hares, (said to give children hare lips), or hunting down black cats.

Heredity: why you are who you are

The baby's sex was decided at the moment of conception. Like the other physical things, height, freckles, an ear for music, even a particular sneeze, sex is part of the chain of heredity that passes these things on from past to present.

They are carried by *chromosomes*.

Every human cell has 23 pairs of chromosomes, except the sperm, which has 23 singles. The egg cell starts off with 23 pairs but leaves one of each pair behind in the ovary, and sets out with 23 singles too. You can probably guess the rest. When egg and sperm become one fertile cell, each single chromosome finds a matching mate waiting for it, so the fertile cell has 23 pairs like all the others.

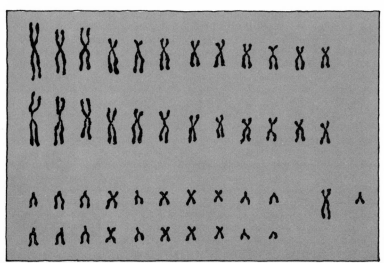

The 23 chromosome pairs of a human male cell. The 23rd pair has two odd ones, an X and a Y.

*Each parent has a different pack of genes. The gene
packs are shuffled, so each child in a family gets a
different set.*

Between them the chromosomes carry 40,000 to 60,000 genes, and it's the genes that carry out heredity's directions. They instruct every cell what it must grow into, and precisely when to do it. For example, fingernail genes are set to start in the 12th week, and in every human foetus, fingernails start growing at 12 weeks.

If every egg and every sperm carried the same genes, children of the same family would be exactly alike, but each egg and each sperm has an entirely different gene mixture, so every child is different.

From one pair of parents there are 70,000,000,000,000 —seventy million million—possible gene combinations, in other words seventy million million possible different children. It makes you realize how special each child is.

How amazing to think that if a particular egg had not been fertilized by a particular sperm at just the right time, there might never have been a you—you are a chance in seventy million million.

Genes are handed on unchanged, and the same ones may crop up anywhere in a family, so a child may be more like an uncle or a grandparent than his brothers and sisters.

Maybe father blames mother's genes for his big-eared children. He could be right or wrong, but when it comes to baby's sex it is *his* chromosomes that decide it and his alone.

The ovum starts with two sex chromosomes, both female—XX—so it doesn't matter which one it sheds in the ovary. The sperm has either an X or a Y chromosome. If the chromosome pairs are XX, then it's a girl, and if XY it's a boy.

The chances of a baby being boy or girl are nearly equal. For every 100 boys born alive there are 106 girls. It seems that a male foetus is more likely to be miscarried than a female.

Family likeness can persist for many generations.

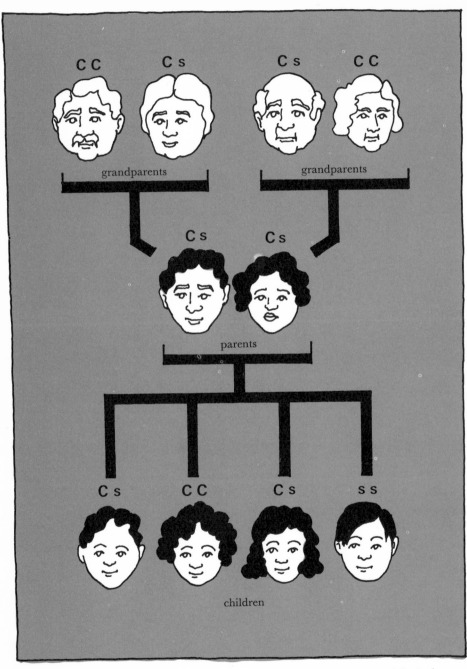

Genes are either dominant or recessive. Curly hair genes are dominant (*c*) and straight hair genes recessive (*s*), so while you need two straight genes (*ss*) to be straight haired, one curly gene (*cs*) is enough to produce curls.

Both parents in this picture inherited a straight gene from one grandparent, and just one of their children has inherited two recessive genes (one from each of them) and has straight hair.

31

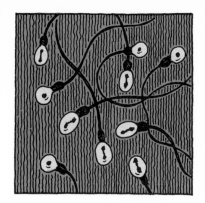

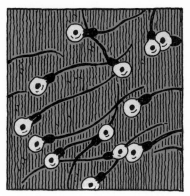

A sperm sample showing the normal mixture of X and Y chromosomes.

A sperm sample said to be from a man whose family produced almost nothing but boys for 256 years. Every sperm would have a Y sex chromosome.

A *miscarriage* happens when a foetus is pushed out of the womb too early to survive. Sometimes it's a way of discarding a foetus that has not grown properly. If it is known that a foetus is damaged then a miscarriage can be produced by a doctor; this is called an *abortion*.

When people are looking forward to a new baby a miscarriage is very sad for them. Luckily it doesn't mean they can't have perfectly healthy children afterwards, and people usually do.

Sometimes children feel they disappointed their parent by not being the right sex. One little girl, tired of hearing how much her parents had wanted a boy, retorted, "Well, I was going to be a boy, but you went on about it so much, I decided to be me instead."

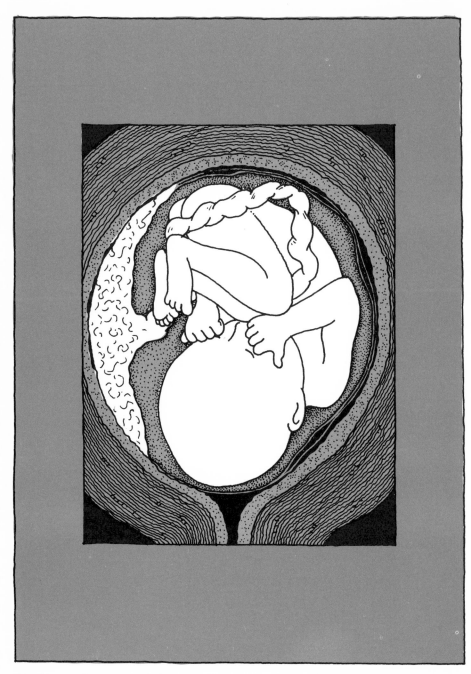

The 14-week foetus—actual size.

14 weeks: quickening

Fourteen weeks after conception the embryo weighs about four ounces/110 g, and is 4–5 in. long/10–12 cm, at this stage the same size as the placenta.

His major development finished, he lies curled round in the womb, arms folded, head bent, legs crossed and knees tucked up. This is known as the "foetal position". Perhaps you curl up like this when you snuggle down to sleep or when you are feeling miserable. Psychiatrists think it comforts us to go back to the shape we had in the safe warm womb.

Certainly some fretful babies are soothed by being wrapped tightly in a shawl and tucked up in a small box. It's thought they feel strange and frightened in the vast spaces around them, after the snug nest of the womb.

33

IM—C

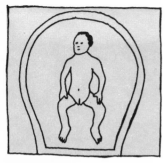

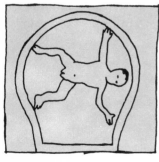

A 15th-century idea of the child's movements in the womb.

As the foetus grows, the womb stretches to fit it and by 14 weeks the womb is so large that it pushes up out of the pelvis.

The baby has been moving since 4 weeks, but when the womb is above the pelvis the mother feels her baby moving for the first time. Now it's a faint fluttering as though a butterfly were in there. It will be stronger later on.

In olden days people thought this movement was life beginning. It was called "the quickening"—quick is an old word for alive, as in the saying "the quick and the dead", which doesn't only apply to those crossing busy roads.

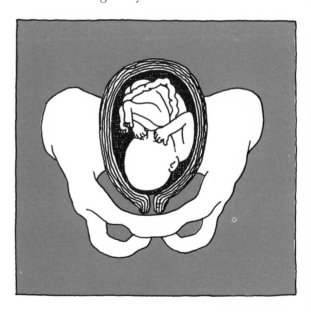

First foetal movements are felt when the womb is so large it rises above the bones of the pelvis. Because of its movements a Balinese mother calls an unborn child her "little caterpillar".

Only women can have babies: what do men feel
about that? This fact can be used to keep women
out of "the man's world" of work and interests, and
keep them busy with housework, nappy changing and
waiting on men. Some men feel very left out, and
envious of woman's creative role. Zeus was so jealous of
his pregnant wife Metis that he swallowed her and
gave birth to the child himself, through the top of
his head. One man said that if he could have the
children he'd give birth to them in three months,
not wait for nine. What do you think about it?

Pregnancy: what's it like?

So far we have talked a lot about the foetus but not much about the two other people concerned—mother and father. What is pregnancy like for them?

It changes life for both of them, but it's bound to affect the mother more because the child grows actually inside her body.

How did they know she was pregnant?

Possibly they suspected it when she missed a period, and the womb failed to shed its lining. After two missed periods they could be fairly sure. They could just wait and see, but often couples ask for a pregnancy test.

The test is done with a test-tube of the woman's morning *urine*, which is mixed with special particles. If she is pregnant the embryo's tissue will be making a *hormone* called "gonadatrophin", which is present in her urine. This hormone makes the special particles stick together or agglutinate.

If the woman is pregnant and the particles stick together they fall in a particular circular pattern at the bottom of the test-tube. If she is not pregnant and there is no gonadatrophin the particles sink down to the bottom and cover it.

The Ancient Egyptians 3,300 years ago knew that urine is changed by pregnancy. They poured it on beans or wheat—if they grew, then the woman was with child.

It wasn't an accurate test, and none was devised until the twentieth century when first rabbits, then rats and toads were used for testing. When these animals were injected with a pregnant woman's urine, the gonadatrophin caused the females to produce eggs, and, with toads, the males to produce sperm. The sort of chemical test described above is quicker and easier to carry out.

Some of the methods used in pregnancy testing.

beans and lentils used by the Ancient Egyptians. The test took several days

20th century Rabbits used for Friedmann test— which took 48 hours

Xenopus toads followed rabbits. Results came after 48 hours provided the toad didn't eat her own eggs

Chemical testing Takes less than 2 hours and is 98% accurate

Once parents know they are expecting a baby their first question is, "When?"

An average pregnancy lasts 266½ days, but it's impossible to give an exact date of birth because conception can happen as long as four days after intercourse. Usually the doctor adds 280 days (40 weeks) to the date of the last period, but it's only a rough sum. One in twelve babies arrives on that date, but one in ten is as much as two weeks before or after ·the date without being either early or late.

A strange but true fact of pregnancy is the longing for particular and sometimes peculiar food that many mothers experience. It may be for marmalade or mutton, and can be for sardine-ice-cream or even bits of coal. It can vary with each child; a mother who ate thousands of raspberries with her first baby may fancy as many anchovies with her second.
Doctors call these longings "pica", Latin for "magpie", a bird known for collecting strange objects.

How does it feel, being pregnant?

Some women feel marvellous, some feel sick at first though this usually wears off after three months. Most of them are a bit worried that something may go wrong, or that they may not be the best person in the world to be a parent.

Usually they slow down, especially in the last months when they are too large to sprint about anyway. Often they feel not only well, but peaceful and happy. This is partly because they are full of vitamins and the sorts of hormone that make you quiet. They are being used as incubators and incubators don't jump about a lot.

Fathers and mothers can spend the months of pregnancy getting used to the idea of a baby arriving, and preparing for it. Fathers can make cots and shelves and the things babies need after birth and, most important, give the mother-to-be lots of moral support. Mothers can make sure the baby gets a good healthy start now. This means eating good food, full of protein, minerals and vitamins—you know the sort of thing, meat and cheese and fish, and lots of fresh fruit and vegetables. She ought to stop smoking, too.

The baby gets first go at nourishment, so if one of them goes short it's mother, but that seems only fair as she controls the diet. Most doctors give extra vitamin and mineral pills to make sure both are fit and well.

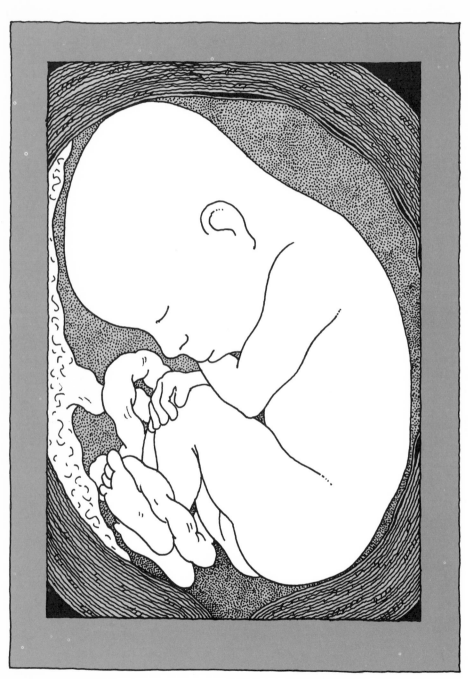

16-week foetus—actual size.

16 weeks: time for hair

Meanwhile, back in the womb, the 16-week foetus is about to put on a spurt of growth.

He is 8–10 in. long/20–25 cm, and weighs about 6 oz/135 g. During the next four weeks he will grow to half his birth height, and at 20 weeks he will be 12 in. long/30 cm and weigh 1 lb/475 g.

His head hair starts growing, and his skin is coated with a white waxy cream called *vernix caseosa*—vernix is the Latin word for varnish. The vernix doesn't really varnish the skin but it does waterproof it. If you have ever spent a long time in water and noticed how your skin wrinkled afterwards, you will realize how important it is for the vernix to protect baby's skin.

As well as his head hair, the baby grows a fine downy hair on the rest of his body. It is called *lanugo*, and it vanishes before he's born. There seems no reason for its appearance and disappearance. Maybe it is a reminder that our ancestors were furry too.

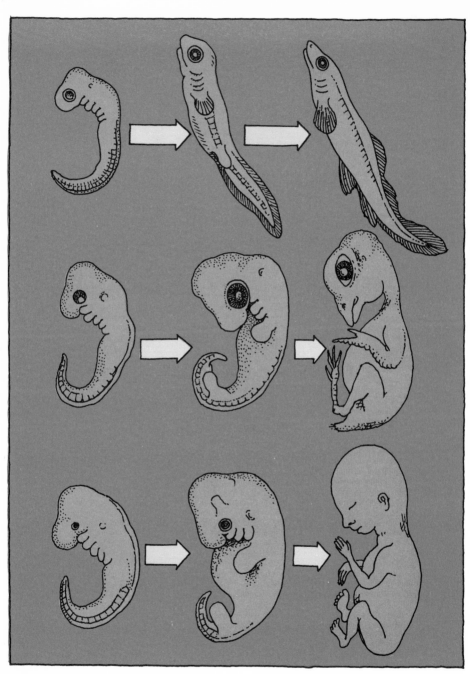

Some scientists have suggested that human embryo's growth follows the same path as evolution, starting as water life and going on through apes to man. These embryos of a fish, a bird and man, (enlarged to the same size) are at the same stages of growth. At first they are all fish-like, with a gill-like structure to the right of the eye. It is still there at the second stage when the limb buds grow. At the third stage it is clear which embryo is which, and only in man have the gills disappeared.

Twins

At 22 weeks the child's heart beats strongly enough to be heard through a stethoscope.

It has been beating since the 4th week, faintly at first, but by 16 weeks it is pumping 50 pints of blood a day, gradually increasing to 600 pints a day on the day of birth.

On or after the 22nd week a doctor may hear through a stethoscope the double heartbeat that is the first sign of twins.

The mother-to-be can hear the heart beats of her own baby (or babies) through this weighted stethoscope.

What causes twins?

Well, there are two kinds; identical twins who are exactly alike, and fraternal twins who may be unalike in everything, except their birthday.

One set of twins in three is identical. They come from a single fertile egg that split into two separate eggs. Each has the same chromosome pairs, so they will be identical in every physical respect, though not in personality.

Fraternal twins are more common—two in every three sets. These twins come from two separate eggs fertilized by two separate sperm, so it's not surprising they are different. Of the fraternal sets, half are girl and boy, and the other half divide equally into sets of two boys and two girls.

Fraternal twins come from two different eggs and two different sperm, so they have different chromosomes and genes. They will not be specially alike, and may be of different sexes.

Identical twins come from a single sperm and a single egg, so they have the same chromosomes and genes. They will look alike and be of the same sex.

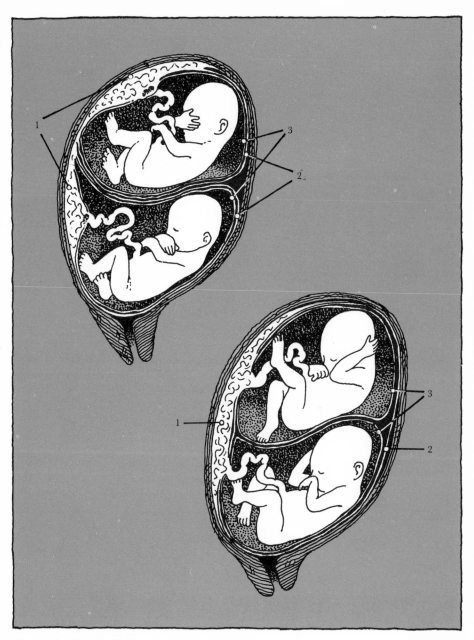

Fraternal twins usually have
  1. Separate placentas
  2. Separate outer bags
  3. Separate inner sacs.

Most identical twins will have
  1. One common placenta
  2. One common outer bag (chorion)
  3. Separate inner sacs (amnions)

Fraternal twins may look very alike because of family likeness; you can tell if they are identical or not by matching their foot and palm prints; those of identical twins are exactly the same.

What are the chances of having twins? On average, one chance in 80, though it's more if there are twins in the family, or if you have twins already.

The chance of three babies at a time—triplets—is one in 80 × 80, of four at a time—quadruplets—one in 80 × 80 × 80, of five at a time—quintuplets—one in 80 × 80 × 80 × 80, and so on.

Multiple births—twins, triplets and so on, are just like other births, but of course the mother is much busier afterwards.

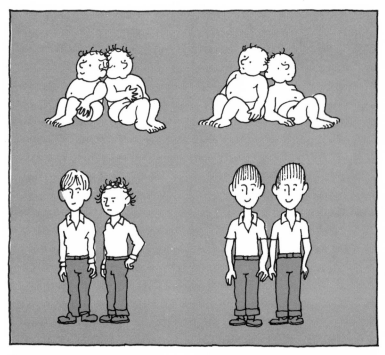

Fraternal twins often look more alike as infants but grow up looking dissimilar.

Identical twins are often less alike as infants, but become more alike as time goes on.

In some places twins are considered magical. The Yoruba of south-west Nigeria believe twins are almost gods and very powerful. There, the first-born twin is said to be the younger, because the older one sent him out to spy out the land.

Yoruba twins must always be treated equally. Should one die, the woodcarver makes a small figure of the same tribe and sex, and the parents give this "ibeji" exactly the same beads and bracelets they give the living twin. If the second twin dies young, another ibeji is carved and dressed in the same way. The Yoruba believe that dead twins stay always young, and play eternally in "the heaven of breezes".

Romulus and Remus, the famous twin brothers who founded Rome in 753 B.C. Said to have been abandoned by cruel parents, they were suckled by a she-wolf until found by a shepherd.

24-week foetus—actual size

24 weeks: the bouncing baby

At 24 weeks the foetus is 14 in./35 cm long, and weighs 1 lb 2 oz/500 g because it's putting on a little fat. Under the buds of the first teeth, which appeared at 11 weeks, the buds of the second teeth are growing in the jaw.

One finishing touch—from now on his eyes are unsealed so he can open and close them.

He is very lively now, bouncing around in the bag of amniotic fluid. Head up or head down, he doesn't seem to mind.

The tremendous jumps he gives can be enough to wake the mother, or even the father if he's right next to her. They can see the child, jumping and bouncing under the mother's skin, and feel tiny hands or feet punching up and out. If they balance a book on the bulge, they will see it quiver and jiggle as the baby exercises inside.

 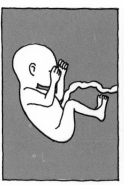 

Between bouts of movement the baby sleeps. All babies have their favourite "lies", and your way of sleeping may be the one you started in the womb.

Used world-wide for at least 1,200 years, this magic word square was supposed to save life during fire and illness as well as childbirth. It could be baked in a cake, or written with butter on bread, and then eaten. During childbirth it was worn round the neck or tied to the right hip.

Old superstition—a needle will swing clockwise over a girl and anticlockwise over a boy. Try it on your friends.

These first outward signs of new life are very moving for parents, and make more real to them the idea of a living child to come.

Mothers especially think and dream about the child inside them. Some think he might be affected by their thoughts and try to have only good and happy ones. They may hope their child will be famous, but the mother of Frank Lloyd Wright went farther than that. When just a few weeks pregnant she decided her baby would be a son, and a great architect, and filled his nursery with pictures of great cathedrals. In fact it was a boy and he did become a world-famous architect.

Parents have tried magic too to keep them and their child safe. Wearing diamonds or emeralds was supposed to stop miscarriage, and the SATOR charm was believed to help in childbirth.

In the 3rd century B.C., the Greek doctor Hippocrates wrote that boys started moving in the womb at 3 months, but the weaker girls didn't get going until 4 months. People believed this in the Middle Ages, and Russian peasants still did at the beginning of this century.

The Chinese think a vigorous foetus is sure to be a girl; the French say late babies must be boys, because boys always hang about instead of getting on.

Of course whichever sex you say the baby is, there is a 50–50 chance you will be right, but many a mother who thought she had a tiny heavyweight champion inside has had a girl, and some quiet little foetuses have become roaring rugby fullbacks. An Israeli doctor carefully wrote down his patients' predictions of boys or girls; most of them were wrong.

An Ashanti girl who wants her baby to be born beautiful will tuck an "Akua ba" doll like this one into her skirt.

26 weeks: the premature baby

By his 26th week the foetus is very human looking, though his head is large in proportion to his body.

He is not as pretty as he might be: his skin is red and wrinkled; his arms and legs are skinny because he has so little body fat, and the silky lanugo hair has not yet disappeared.

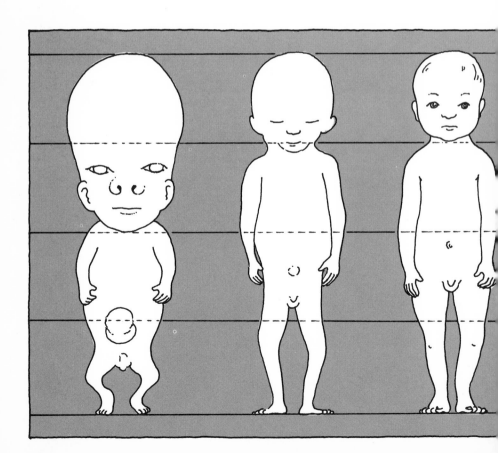

Do you know what a *premature baby* is?

It's a baby born before its full time in the womb is ended.

A 26-week baby can suck a little, and his lungs are developed enough for breathing, so a baby born after the 26th week still has a chance of survival.

How is a premature baby cared for?

He's not really ready for life outside, and while he can breathe, he's not very good at it, and he's rather drowsy too, so often he is given oxygen.

If his sucking isn't strong enough, he is fed by tube, either in his mouth or nose. If his sucking is good he is fed with a special bottle that gives extra large mouthfuls. He needs feeding every 2 or 3 hours, day and night, to keep him going.

These pictures show how body proportions change from those of the embryo to the fully mature adult.

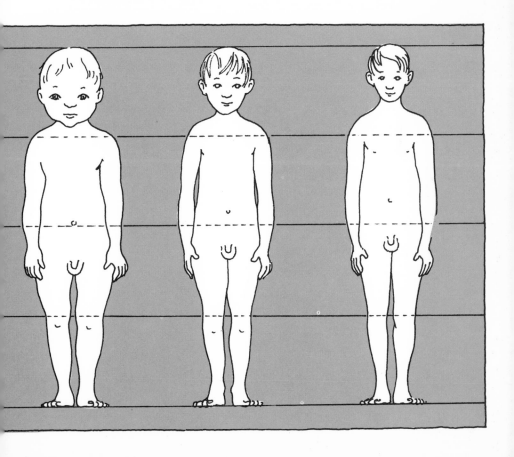

The portholes of an incubator have tightly fitting sleeves, so the baby can be tended with no loss of warmth or risk of infection.

The smallest surviving premature baby was Marion Chapman, at 10 oz/275 g. She was fed hourly with a fountain-pen filler, and weighed 13 lbs.4 ozs/4.97 kg at 1 year.

The heaviest newborn baby ever was Turkish, and weighed in at 24 lbs/10.88 kg.

Since he lacks fat to keep him warm, and he has a poor circulation, he is usually put in an incubator. It's a glass box, where he is kept in warm moist air, about 70°F/21°C, safe from germs and infection. Because he is so tiny—only 2 lbs/850 g —even the weight of clothes might hinder his breathing, and he is left naked in the incubator.

He is watched carefully every hour day and night. As he grows stronger and larger he is moved to an ordinary cot in a warm nursery, and if all goes well his parents can take him home when he weighs 5½ lbs/2.5 kg.

If a new baby stays in hospital it is important for parents to see him all the time, and, whenever possible, hold him and cuddle him. Though a premature baby is tiny and seems barely alive, he's beginning the important process called "imprinting". He has to get to know the look, the sound, the feel, the smell, everything about his mother particularly. The better he knows her, the stronger his imprinting, and the safer and happier he will feel.

Premature babies are sometimes a little behind "full term" babies, but as they are really younger than they seem they ought not to be compared with children of their own age. In time they catch up completely and no one can tell the difference.

Several stories have tiny heroes or heroines, e.g. Thumbelina and Tom Thumb. Being a dwarf or a midget is nothing to do with being premature. The smallest recorded adult was a Dutch girl of 24 in./60 cm —the average length of a newborn baby is 20.5 in./51.2cm.

Their "imprinting" has made ducklings treat this man as their mother. He quacked to them in the shell and took care of them after hatching and now they follow him everywhere. Here he teaches them to fly by running and flapping his arms; they imitate and take off successfully.

The 30-week foetus—actual size.

30-34 weeks: presentation

Between the 26th and 34th weeks the foetus will grow 8–10 in./ 20–25 cm, and put on lots of weight. The fat makes his skin smooth and white instead of red and wrinkled, and keeps him warm after birth. It brings his weight up to around 4½–6 lbs/2–2.75 kg.

At 28 weeks, when his head hair starts growing fast, he sheds the lanugo. At this stage he may enjoy sucking his thumb or finger, and may even cry when he can't. Some babies arrive with thumbs marked by long sucking. His fingernails are growing so fast that by the time he is born they will probably need trimming.

By the 30th week the baby is about 18 in./45 cm long and weighs about 5½ lbs/2.5 kg. If he is lying more quietly than before, arms folded and knees tucked up, it's only because there is not enough room for his old antics. If his mother overeats he will be so chubby he won't be able to move at all.

58

In the 34th week, a month before birth, the baby takes his final position in the womb and waits to be born. The best position for birth is head straight down, but some babies have heads down with forehead or face first. Other babies sit down to be born, or lie right across the womb putting their foot or shoulder first. If there is enough room, the baby can be turned round by the gentle pushings of a midwife or doctor, but a lot of babies, carefully turned right way down, wriggle back to their old position after a day or two.

There is an antenatal technique called "decompression", where the mother is put into a sort of inflatable space suit. It is blown up until the pressure of the suit is the same as that inside her body. When the pressures are equalized, there is little or no pressure on the foetus and its blood can circulate more freely than before. Some say better circulation brings more oxygen and food for the growing child, though not everyone agrees decompression does this.

One of the few new events at this time is the passing of *antibodies* (gamma globulin) from mother to baby. These antibodies will protect him from illnesses

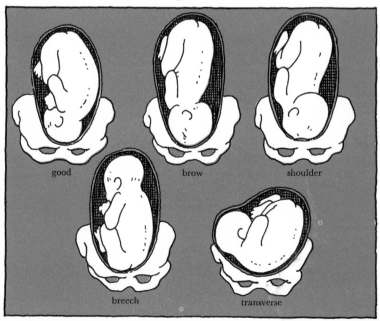

Various birth positions or "presentations".

that his mother has had or been injected against. This immunity from disease lasts six months, and by then the baby's blood will have built up its own resistance. The antibodies are missed by premature babies, which is why they need to lie in incubators to protect them from infection.

During the last months of pregnancy women are encouraged to do exercises which help them to relax and to cope with the pains of the birth. Here a father is timing his wife's breathing exercises.

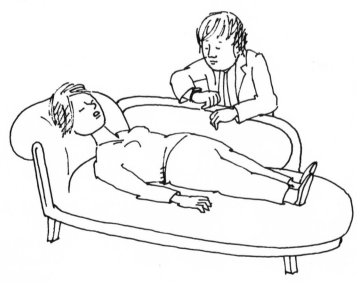

36 weeks: engagement

Another unlikely picture of Ambroise Paré's shows "Dorothea", said to have had 9 babies in her first pregnancy and 11 in her second, easing the weight of her huge abdomen with a wooden hoop slung from her shoulders.

Two weeks before birth, the 36th week of life, the foetus is a perfect baby. All his organs are working, and he's practising breathing and swallowing and sucking. He has enough fat to keep him warm, and hair on his head. Whatever race he is, his eyes are bluish now, though they change slowly to their proper colour after birth. He gains more weight in proportion to body size than he will for the rest of his life. Mother, too, reaches her largest ever size, with a record waist—or what was once a waist—of about 40 in./100 cm instead of an average 26 in./65 cm. People tease her, and say, "When did you last see your feet?" and it's true she has to make a special effort to do so. She is often rather uncomfortable and feels squashed inside, her walk is a waddle and clothes that fit her are more like tents than dresses. Keeping up pants is a problem, they must be well above the bulge, or they shimmer down.

The last two weeks of pregnancy are more comfortable for her when the baby's head slides down into the pelvic girdle for the final birth position. This is called the "engaging" of the head. It lets the womb sink down about 2 in./5 cm in the mother's body, so everything else has a little more space.

The sensation of relief is so noticeable and so pleasant that this stage is called the *"lightening"*.

The baby is at his largest now, about 20 in./50 cm long and $7\frac{1}{2}$ lbs/3.5 kg in weight. He is wedged tightly in the uterus with little room to move, so his mother feels only a few faint flutters as she and he wait for his birthday.

During the last six days the baby scarcely grows. The placenta which gave him nourishment for most of the nine months changes over to making chemicals. These will start off *labour*, the process that will push him out of the womb and into the world.

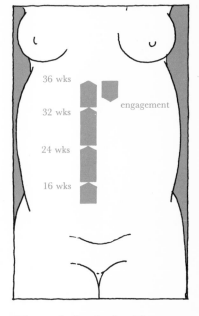

The womb rises in the abdomen until the "lightening" when it descends 2 in./5 cm.

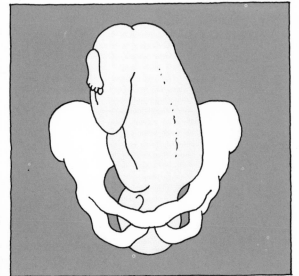

Engagement. The baby's head slides right down into the pelvic girdle.

The first nine months of life

7 days old. The fertilized egg implants itse[lf] in the womb.

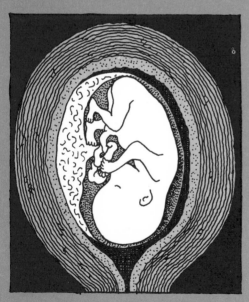

12 weeks old; weight 1 oz/28 g, its basic structure is finished and its sex distinguishable.

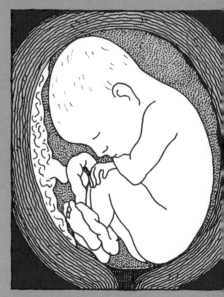

16 weeks old; 6 ozs/135 g in weight; he moves freely. The lanugo grows and head h[air]. The placenta is almost finished.

...s old, and 10,000 times the size of the ...lls. Its arms and leg buds grow and its ...eats. The placenta starts to form.

8 weeks old; the foetus has a face, arms, hands and fingers, legs, feet and toes, and a skeleton of soft gristle.

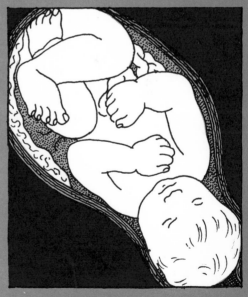

...ks old; weight 18 ozs/1 kg, and more ...alf his birth height, he is very lively. ...f second teeth grow under those of the ...eth.

38 weeks old; weight 7½ lbs/3.5 kg, the perfect baby waits to be born.

The first stage of labour

What starts everything moving?

A head-hunting tribe called the Iatmul believe the child decides when to be born.

The gentler Arapesh of New Guinea think the baby sleeps through nine months, wakens when it's time to be born, then dives out of the womb like a swimmer.

The famous Doctor Harvey who discovered the circulation of blood in 1628 thought a child fought its own way out. Nowadays, though we know much more about the process of labour, we still don't know everything.

The process is called "labour" because it's hard work, for the mother and for the womb. It begins when the baby is getting too large for the womb, but is still small enough to go through the narrow birth passage.

When the hormones and chemicals made by the placenta begin to affect the uterus, it starts its work. It must do two things, open itself, and push out the baby; and it does them both at once.

First it pushes the baby down, hard, and that does mean hard. The pressure of these pushes can be 55 lbs to the square inch/4 kgs to the square cm. It makes him straighten up, and forces his head against the neck of the womb, the *cervix*. This was sealed during pregnancy, but now its plug of skin comes out, so when the uterus presses down at the top and pulls up at the sides, the cervix opens wider and wider.

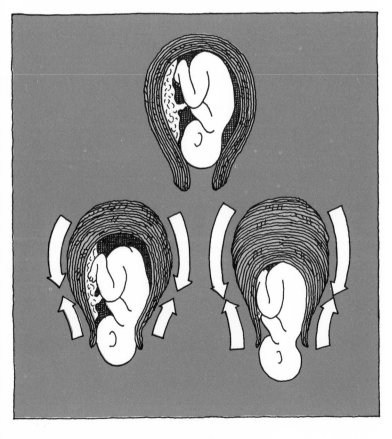

The uterus pulls itself UP at the sides, and presses DOWN on top. Its sides get shorter and the top thicker as it pushes the baby out.

These clenchings of the womb are called *contractions*. If you put a hand on the mother's abdomen you would feel it grow hard and tight, then soft again as the contraction faded. The first contractions last only a few seconds, and have gaps between as long as half an hour. They get closer together and last longer. When they are happening every fifteen or twenty minutes it's time to set off for the hospital.

The contractions continue, the uterus goes on pressing and pulling, pressing and pulling, making the cervix open wider and wider. When the first stage is almost over, the amnion breaks and the amniotic fluid rushes out with a great gush. It's called "the breaking of the waters", and is usually a sign that the next contractions will send the baby's head through the cervix into the birth passage, and the second stage of labour. At this time the cervix has a diameter of about $3\frac{3}{4}$ in./9.5 cm.

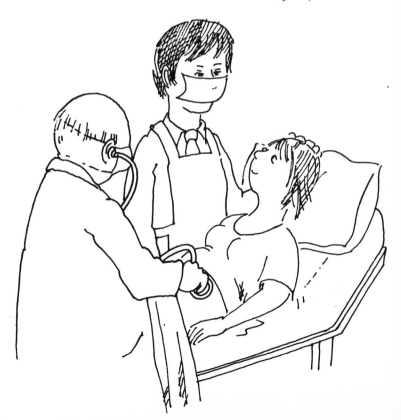

A midwife is a nurse who specializes in delivering babies. In the old days women were denied the services of educated doctors, and doctors refused to educate the midwives. On the rare occasion when a doctor was called in, he could inspect only the woman's face and hands and delivered the baby under a blanket. 16th-century midwives were said to dabble in witchcraft, charming the mother's pains into dogs or cats. The Church insisted that a midwife's ability to baptize a child was more important than her competence or cleanliness. By the early 19th century, when one mother in 100 died in childbirth, women themselves insisted on more adequate care, and the next century saw more scientific and educational progress than ever before.

The first part of labour can last a long time—48 hours or so, but the mother can help herself by relaxing properly between contractions and getting as much rest as she can, and the father can help by rubbing her back and keeping her company. The relaxation between is important for the baby, because when a contraction squeezes the placenta, baby's head is moving out through the cervix, and into the birth canal for the second stage and he gets less oxygen.

A birth stool, very common in Europe.

When the first stage of labour is over the father and mother know their baby is two hours away at most.

In Western countries most mothers lie down for the baby's birth, but as these pictures show, this isn't always the case.

Labour in Loango.

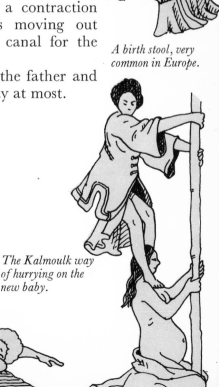

The Kalmoulk way of hurrying on the new baby.

Does it hurt? Anaesthetics

morel
(mushroom)
hemlock
lettuce
mulberries
poppy
mandrake

Crusader's recipe for the "sleeping sponge" given to wounded soldiers.

One question we all want to ask, though we don't always like to, is—"Does it hurt?"

Perhaps you have read a story or seen a film where the heroine gives birth, writhing in pain and agony, and sometimes dying in the attempt. It's true childbirth can be painful, but most films and books are produced by people with no actual experience. The pain of childbirth is special too, because it's not the pain of illness and there will be something to show for it at the end.

Children sometimes worry in case they hurt their mother when they were born. In fact they did nothing, just lay there being sent out. Anyway, the pain of childbirth is pushed aside by joy, and forgotten completely.

Nowadays many women practise "natural childbirth". Because they know what's happening and what to do they are not afraid, and can relax through their contractions. If any woman has too much pain she can always ask for anaesthetics (pain-killing drugs) and everything is done to make her comfortable.

Earlier in history they thought a woman couldn't love her child unless she suffered for it, so her pain was considered a good thing. On the other hand men in

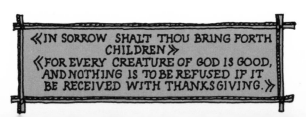

《IN SORROW SHALT THOU BRING FORTH CHILDREN 》
《FOR EVERY CREATURE OF GOD IS GOOD, AND NOTHING IS TO BE REFUSED IF IT BE RECEIVED WITH THANKSGIVING.》

pain were cared for; gladiators and soldiers were given sleeping sponges to lessen the pains of their wounds. When the anaesthetics *ether* and *chloroform* were discovered in the nineteenth century, there was uproar when doctors suggested using them for women in labour. James Simpson of Edinburgh was the first doctor to try them. One woman was so grateful to him, she called her baby girl Anaesthesia.

Wilhelmina Anaesthesia Carstairs, the first child whose mother had pain-killing drugs during delivery. Simpson had her picture on his study wall.

Many women refused anaesthetics for childbirth, until, in 1852, Queen Victoria used them for the birth of Prince Leopold. After that lots of people changed their minds.

It is interesting that while Simpson had modern ideas about anaesthetics, he thought the new ideas of cleanliness stopping spread of infection were rather far-fetched.

Snow's portable chloroform inhaler, an early form of anaesthetic used in childbirth.

Queen Victoria was a pioneer in the use of anaesthesia in childbirth, and also had one of the first-ever woman doctors— Marianne Siebald of Bavaria.

Second stage of labour. Head out of the uterus, the baby must go through the narrow birth canal before emerging into the world.

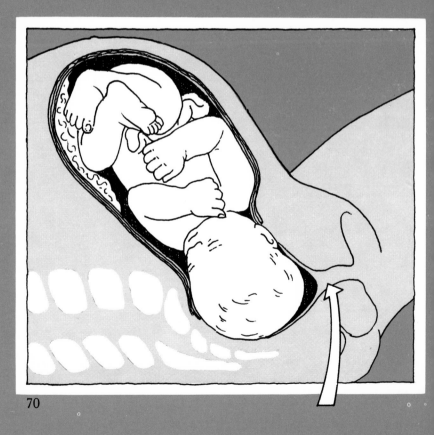

The second stage of labour: born at last

During the second stage of labour the baby is pushed along the birth canal and out. It is a hard push because the passage is narrow, and curves up at the end. To send the baby along, a pressure of about 100 lbs to the square inch (7.3 kgs to the square cm) is needed, so the mother must add her push to the womb's contractions.

The passage is tightest round the baby's head, his widest part. Luckily the skull bones are not yet joined, so there is some "give" in his head. The plates of bone can slide together or even overlap without harming his brain.

This explains how such a large baby can come out, and also all those jokes you hear about pointed heads. The baby's head may be elongated after birth, but it settles back into a normal rounded shape. The bone plates don't fuse until 6 months after birth, and many books suggest a baby sleeps on alternate sides to keep his head symmetrical.

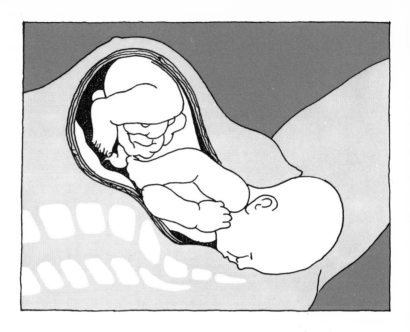

The head is "crowned".

The contractions in the second stage of labour are much stronger, and closer together. There is a sense of urgency about them now. The mother helps with her pushes, and gives a good grunt as she does so. This stage is fairly exhausting for her, and the father and the doctors and nurses give her lots of encouragement.

With each push the baby is closer to being born, slipping back a little as the contraction fades. One push sends the baby so far along that the doctor sees the top of his head. It slips back; but a few hard pushes later the head comes right out. The baby's head is "crowned".

Usually the baby comes out face down, but the next contraction, which brings out his shoulder, spins him right round to face upwards. He needs no more pushes, the rest of him just swooshes out—and there he is—born.

First sight of the baby's head.

As the shoulders come out, the baby is spun round.

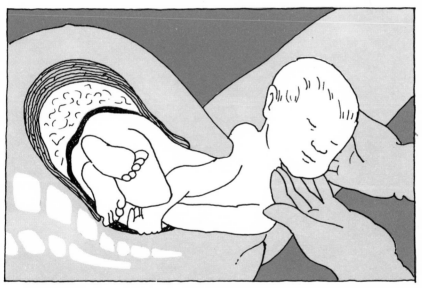

There he is—born.

There is no other moment quite like it, when parents see their new child for the very first time.

"It's a girl."

"It's a boy."

"Is it all right?"

All the waiting, the work and the worry are over, all the pain and the mess is past and forgotten as they hold their child in their arms. It's like falling in love at first sight, seeing this stranger who is not a stranger, but one of the family.

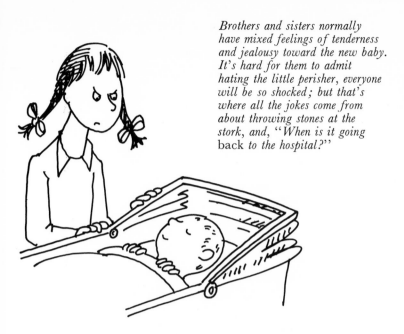

*Brothers and sisters normally
have mixed feelings of tenderness
and jealousy toward the new baby.
It's hard for them to admit
hating the little perisher, everyone
will be so shocked; but that's
where all the jokes come from
about throwing stones at the
stork, and, "When is it going
back to the hospital?"*

Mind you, he's not much to look at. The doctor will have cleared any mucus from his mouth so his breathing is clear, but otherwise he is just as he was in the womb. His skin may be wrinkled and bluish, he'll be coated with the waxy vernix caseosa, and streaked here and there with blood. His head may be elongated and his face furrowed, but to his parents he's the most beautiful thing in the world—which is just as it ought to be. Sometimes people have not wanted a child particularly, until they saw it—there's a saying, "they bring their own love with them", and it's often true.

*Chinese babies start life at 1 year
old, because their pre-birth life is
counted as their first year.*

The third stage of labour

In all this excitement and happiness the third stage of labour happens almost unnoticed. Once the baby is born and starts breathing he does not need the placenta, and its circulation stops. When the umbilical cord stops pulsing, it's cut (this doesn't hurt at all). Usually a clip is put on the bit left behind, which dries up and falls off after about a week, leaving behind its lifetime scar, the *navel* or belly-button.

The umbilicus is cut (it doesn't hurt), and is tied or clipped. Nigerian babies are then shaken three times to make them strong and fearless, and touched on the ground to save them pain when falling.

The third stage of labour is carefully watched by the doctors. It is the few contractions needed to push out the placenta—then called the *afterbirth*, which looks like a piece of raw liver.

76

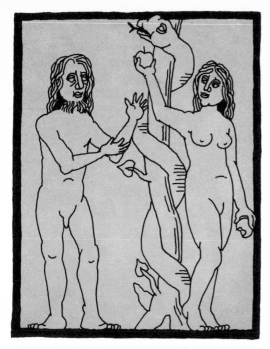

Adam and Eve, the only people never to have navels— they were created by God and not born. One of the arguments for anaesthesia was that God put Adam into a deep sleep before removing the rib from which Eve was made.

With the last contraction, the empty womb starts returning to normal, from its present 12 in./30 cm-long vegetable marrow shape to its usual 3 in./$7\frac{1}{2}$ cm pear shape. It will go on shrinking; the mother will feel it as "after pains"; slight twinges not lasting very long, during the next few days.

When the after-birth has arrived the mother is usually washed and freshened up, then she and the father can hold the baby in their arms and relax after a job well done—in Britain, they are sure to get a "nice cup of tea".

"Born lucky"—for thousands of years the rare child born with a caul (some amnion) over its head, has been said to be lucky. The caul has been used in witches' spells and medicine, worn in a locket, and even eaten, to bring luck. It was widely believed to protect the wearer from drowning, perhaps because the foetus never drowns in the amnion, and was very popular with sailors. During the Napoleonic wars British sailors paid £30 each for them. Prices fell off in the early twentieth century to just a few shillings, but when war broke out in 1914 prices soared to the £5 mark.

Difficult births

The birth described here is the normal one that happens nearly every time, but things can go differently or even wrong. The baby may come early. Second babies often arrive fast, occasionally in taxis or ambulances on their way to hospital. The main thing is to keep the baby warm, wrap it up with the afterbirth—no need to worry about cutting the cord, that can be done later.

A "breech birth", when a baby comes out bottom first, may need to be pulled from outside as well as pushed from inside. This is done with *forceps*—a nasty sharp sounding word, but they are long curved tongs of smooth steel which can hold the baby, and gently but firmly bring him out.

This breech birth baby is helped out gently but firmly with forceps. Mother and baby are both safe and unharmed.

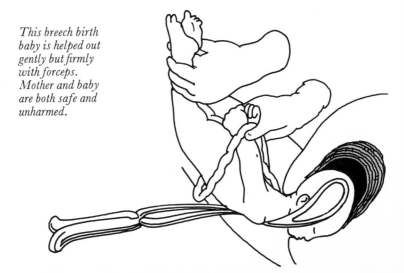

Forceps were once a great mystery. They were invented by the Chamberlens, a family of French Huguenot doctors, who fled from France in 1572. Every woman wanted to be delivered by the Chamberlens, because of their secret weapon, which made labour shorter and easier.

The Chamberlens always arrived with a carved and gilded box, so heavy it had to be carried by two servants. The patient was blindfolded, the midwife sent away, the door locked. A slapping of sticks was heard and a ringing of bells. This noise hid the clinking of the forceps with which they helped out the unborn child. The Chamberlens kept their secret for more than 100 years.

Foreceps are useful if a child has a large head, or the mother a small pelvis. Sometimes a vacuum extractor is used to grip the baby's head—that too is perfectly safe for mother and child.

In between 1 per cent and 5 per cent of births the woman's pelvic girdle is very small, so her baby may have difficulty in getting out. The doctors tell the parents it is best for their baby to be born by *Caesarian section*.

This means the baby is taken out through the abdomen. The mother is given a complete anaesthetic, and her abdomen is cut to make an opening large enough for baby and afterbirth to be removed by hand. Her abdomen is very large at the time, but after the operation only a small scar remains.

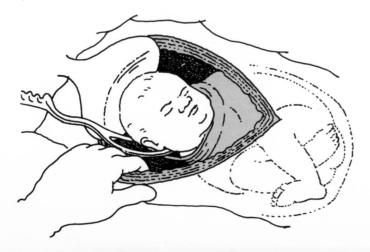

First sight of a baby born by Caesarian section. He will be carefully lifted out and the afterbirth removed by hand.

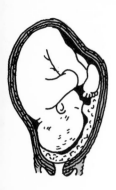

Occasionally the egg implants itself at the bottom of the womb and the placenta grows there. A normal delivery might mean a dead or damaged baby so, for this "placenta previa" baby, a Caesarian section will be best.

The Caesarian section is also used for a baby distressed by a long labour; a doctor can easily tell by listening to the baby's heart. It's useful too where the placenta is at the bottom of the womb, "placenta previa", or for a baby lying awkwardly, if he cannot be turned. It is not as alarming as it sounds, and saves many babies who might otherwise be born dead or damaged.

The operation is named after Julius Caesar; he wasn't born this way, but his law, "lex caesaria", allowed doctors to remove the unborn children of dead or dying mothers like this. Unfortunately the operation was never successful, until 1500, when Jacob Nufer delivered his wife's baby by Caesarian section. His wife had six more children, including a pair of twins, and the baby lived to be 77.

Version, which means turning, is used for babies with difficult presentations. They are turned during the second stage of labour so that their feet or their head can be delivered first.

This chapter tells you some difficulties of childbirth; there may be dangerous moments, but modern medical care makes it safer to have a baby than crossing a busy street.

Niam-Niam women give birth alone on a birth stool, but are given a musical accompaniment, perhaps for moral support.

In many parts of the world birth is a "girls only" affair. Some primitive women even go off alone to have their child.

In other places there is "couvade": when the husband is supposed to feel the pains of childbirth, so his wife can produce their baby painlessly. Around 1270 Marco Polo saw women of Chinese Turkestan return to work the minute they had their baby, leaving it tucked up with the husband, who rested 40 days after his hard labours. Today in South America a Waiani Indian rocks in his hammock and groans loudly, believing he takes on his wife's pains. Perhaps, if she believes it won't hurt, it won't, so it does help her. Who knows?

Today more and more fathers see their children born. Mothers say it comforts them, and many couples find this shared experience brings them closer together, but some poor fathers are still hustled off, and miss the birth.

Midwives in the Middle Ages thought men would go off women for life if they saw a birth; those were the days when doctors delivered babies under the blankets because it wasn't right for them to see naked women. They had to guess how she was doing from the look of her hands and face.

A Waiani father in labour.

IM—F

What's it like for the baby?

How does the baby feel about being born? What's it like for him? No one remembers their own birth, but we know his first breaths need five times as much effort as ordinary breaths, because his lungs are new. His body, like a new car, must be "run in".

He sees his first light after the darkness of the womb, but he can't focus his eyes yet and the shapes he sees are blurred, and for the first few days, upside down too.

He may be aware of the change in temperature. However cosy his room, it can scarcely compare with the steady 98·4°F/37°C of the mother's womb.

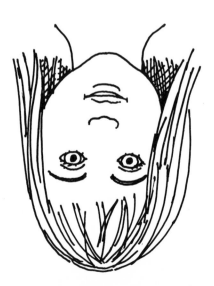

The New Testament tells us how the newly born Jesus was wrapped in swaddling clothes and laid in a manger. Until late in the 18th century most babies were "swaddled", that is, wrapped tightly in bandages, to keep out "bad air" and keep in "nourishing juices" (whatever they were). Changing the nappy of a swaddled baby was considered a dangerous undertaking.

He finds noises very loud and sudden. He's been used to a regular rhythm of heart beats and breathing, with perhaps a background rumble or two. Now they are missing, and there are loud noises which make him jump almost out of his skin. They say most women carry babies on the left, perhaps unconsciously letting the sound of heart beats soothe the child. One Japanese doctor made a record of the sounds an unborn child hears; it's said to be an instant soother for fretful infants. Certainly piglets in incubators do better when tapes of sows' heart beats are played to them, and we know that birds chirp to their chicks while still in the shell, so there may be something in it.

The new baby

A new baby can cry, and very often does, but in the first weeks his eyes have no tears. He makes swimming and crawling movements when he's laid on his stomach. and he can grip amazingly strongly, hard enough to hang from two of your fingers. That may go back to ape ancestors whose children must grip on to mother's fur as they feed. His toes, too, have the same gripping reflex.

crawling and gripping

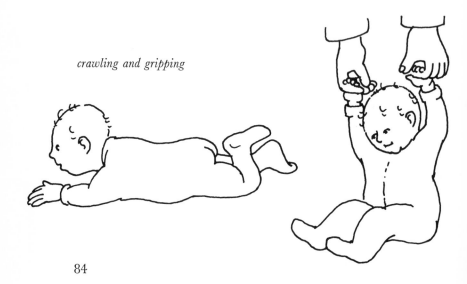

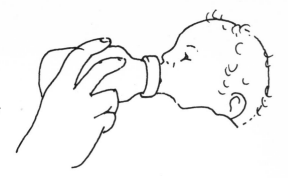

What he's really good at is sucking. . . .

What the baby's really good at is sucking. His little cheeks are fat with the sucking pads inside, and so sensitive that the softest brush of a finger starts him nuzzling and rooting for food. If he's hungry he frets and cries and smacks his lips, but as soon as he gets the breast or bottle, he snaps on to it and sucks away. Sometimes he's so happy and relaxed after a short suck that he falls asleep and has to be woken up again— tickling the soles of his feet is a good way to do it.

One of the first things parents like to do is name their baby. Names have special meanings—do you know the meaning of yours? Most races or religions have special naming ceremonies for a new child. A Bornu baby becomes a person only when named at nine days old. Before that it's always called "little kitten", in case it dies, because the Bornu believe cats and peacocks are the only animals allowed to enter heaven.

New beginnings

The one cell has become two hundred billion. The long process of foetal development is done, the parents' nine months of preparation and waiting are over, the baby is here.

Their friends say about them, "Oh, did you hear, the So-and-Sos have got a new baby?" What they have is not just a new baby, it's a new person; because this baby didn't ask to be born, but is here, willy-nilly, the beginning of a person.

Just now he needs his parents for everything, food, warmth and shelter for survival, and love and interest to make him a human being. But every day will take him further from these parents, closer to a life of his own, quite separate from theirs, part of the new generation who will live on in a world they will never see.

We can't guess what his life will be, but we can be fairly sure that one day he will ask—

"Mother, where did I come from?"

Glossary

Amnion the tough inner bag of skin containing the foetus

Amniotic fluid a fluid made by the amnion in which the baby floats

Abortion the shedding of the foetus too early for it to survive. It can be induced by a doctor, or can happen naturally, in which case it is called a miscarriage

Antenatal before birth

Antibodies blood cells that ingest (eat up) germs, saving the body from illness

Afterbirth the placenta and womb-lining, pushed out of the womb after the child is born

Anaesthesia painkilling drugs. A general anaesthetic puts one right 'out'

Breech birth a baby sitting down to be born, so that it comes out foot or bottom first

Caesarian section an operation in which the baby is taken out through the wall of the abdomen

Cervix the neck of the womb

Chorion the outer lining of the womb, outside the amnion

Chromosome carrier of the 'genes', which transmit physical characteristics

88

Contraception 'family planning': avoiding unwanted conception and so having only the children one wants

Contractions the muscular clenchings of the womb which push the baby out at birth

Embryo the unborn, unfinished child

Engagement the sinking down of the baby's head into the pelvic girdle two weeks before birth

Fallopian tube the narrow tube linking ovary and womb

Fertile able to produce life

Forceps rather like curved tongs; used to help out babies during difficult births

'Full-term' baby a baby who has spent the full nine months in the womb and is not born prematurely

Genes pass on family likeness, abilities, physical characteristics, sex height, colouring etc.

Gamma-globulin the chemical from which antibodies are made (see antibodies)

Hormone a chemical message made by one cell, and sent, via the bloodstream, to another cell, causing it to react

Incubator a glass box in which the premature baby is kept warm and safe from infection

Imprinting the way in which, through close contact, a child gets to know and feel safe with his parents—especially his mother

Labour the process that expels the child from the womb and along the birth canal

Lanugo fine, silky hair which grows on the 20-week foetus, but disappears before birth.

Lightening the sensation of relief that mother has after 'engagement'

Menstruation monthly shedding of the womb lining which has been prepared in case an egg is fertilized

Miscarriage see 'abortion'

Morula the bundle of embryonic cells before implantation (from the Latin word for 'mulberry')

Navel belly button: the scar left by the umbilical cord

Ovum female egg cell

Ovaries produce the female egg cells

Period see 'menstruation'

Pica the longing for particular foods felt sometimes during pregnancy

Placenta the mass of cells which take nourishment from the mother's blood and pass it to the baby

Placenta previa occurs when the placenta grows at the bottom of the womb instead of the top

Premature baby one born before its full time in the womb is up

Presentation the position of the child ready for birth

Quickening the first foetal movement felt by the mother

Sperm (spermatozoa) male cells which fertilize female eggs

Testes male organs in which sperm are made and stored

Umbilicus (umbilical cord) the cord attaching the foetus to the placenta. Blood circulates along it

Uterus womb; pear-shaped female organ in which the foetus grows until birth

Vernix caseosa white waxy cream which waterproofs the foetus in the womb

Version the antenatal turning of the baby to a good birth position

Womb see 'uterus'

Index